Jesus'
TEN
COMMANDMENTS
for
COUPLES

GLOVER SHIPP

 COLLEGE PRESS PUBLISHING CO.
JOPLIN, MISSOURI

*To all of those couples who take seriously this study
and who sign the pledge at the end of the course,
or who frame one of their own,
and prayerfully follow it.*

Copyright © 2002
Glover Shipp

Published by College Press Publishing Co.
On the web at www.collegepress.com

Cover design by Brett Lyerla

International Standard Book Number 0-89900-846-1

FOREWORD

Today, couples are searching for hope, candor, and helpful information to make their marriages work. Glover Shipp has written a wonderful resource for all couples to meet that need.

Ten Commandments for Couples is practical and straight to the point. Glover opens his own marriage and draws upon years of experience.

Dr. Shipp believes marriage is much more than a license; it is a spiritual covenant. He encourages us to speak kindly to our mates, remember special days, and remain faithful. I read it at one sitting and you will enjoy reading it, too.

Don W. Hebbard, Ed.D., Director
Institute for Marriage and Family
Oklahoma Christian University

CONTENTS

2000 AND BEYOND
STUDIES FOR SMALL GROUPS

In pursuit of our stated goal, "Every Christian a Bible Student," College Press has, since 1995, been publishing a series of *Studies for Small Groups*. These have proved very popular, both for group and individual study on a variety of topics and Scripture texts. Although, with the year 2000, we have changed the outward appearance of these study booklets, our commitment is still to providing solid, thought-provoking studies that will make a life-changing difference in the reader.

Of course, although we call these studies "for small groups," they are equally suited for individual study. If you are simply reading the book for your own benefit, please do take the time to use the "Reflecting on . . ." questions to focus your own thoughts. In a small group study, the questions should not only be used as a review, to see if you remember what was actually said in that lesson by the writer, but to help spark discussion of the further *implications* of the lesson material. Nor should you consider the questions that are provided the only questions to be asked. Any study is only as good as the effort you put into it, and the group leader should have read the lesson through thoroughly before the class meets, as well as encouraging all other members of the group to do so if possible. If the leader has gone through the lesson in advance, he or she will probably have thought of other questions, some of which may never have even occurred to the writer or editors of the study. After all, what is important is not just the bare facts of the lesson, but how they intersect with your own path in the Christian walk.

Above all, do not feel you have to race through the lessons. Although the number of lessons is purposely kept small so that no one has to commit in advance to an endless period of time on the study, you should not cut off discussion of an important issue just to fit the whole of the lesson into one study session. Nor do you want to leave off the end of a lesson because you didn't get it all in during the allotted time. The greatest advantage of the small group setting is the flexibility you have, allowing you to carry over discussion to the next session. Take full advantage of this flexibility.

TEN COMMANDMENTS FOR COUPLES

"No rules; just right!" So say the commercials for a popular steak house. We live in a day when "no rules" appears to be the norm. Each person considers himself or herself pretty much autonomous.

This mentality is carried into the workplace, the school, the church, and even the home. Although probably no one enters marriage planning to fail, the prevailing notion is that if it doesn't work out, there is no law to keep a couple from divorcing.

Yet there are laws. We all live under civil law, for instance. The Roman centurion who asked Jesus to heal his servant recognized the principle of authority. He said to Jesus,

> Lord, I do not deserve to have you come under my roof. But just say the word, and my servant will be healed. For I myself

am a man under authority, with soldiers under me. I tell this one, 'Go,' and he goes; and that one, 'Come,' and he comes. I say to my servant, 'Do this,' and he does it (Matt. 8:8-9).

Jesus commended the centurion for his faith. He also emphasized the necessity of living under law. When he was confronted with a loaded question about paying or not paying tribute to the Roman government, he answered, ". . . give to Caesar what is Caesar's, and to God what is God's" (Luke 20:20-25).

God gave us the greatest and most comprehensive set of principles ever revealed. In the Old Testament they are called the Ten Commandments or simply the Law. In the New Testament they are a set of spiritual standards that go to the heart of our attitude, and not just to outward acts. Living by the words of Matthew 5 can enrich our lives, improve our marriages, and prepare us for eternity.

It occurred to me that in our day of casual attitude toward the laws and principles which can keep us in tune with God and our mates, a modern parallel to the Ten Commandments in the book of Exodus might be helpful. What follows in this book, therefore, are Ten Commandments for couples: rules which, if followed, can only reinforce and improve our marriages. Study them, and if you find practical value there, incorporate them into your own marital and family life. Profitable reading!

Glover Shipp
Edmond, Oklahoma

ACKNOWLEDGMENTS

I want to especially thank Charlotte Burrough and Dr. Paul Coffman, dedicated family counselors and colleagues in the Lord's work with the Edmond, Oklahoma, Church of Christ, who read the manuscript and offered valuable suggestions. I am thankful to Dr. Don Hebbard, director of the Institute of Marriage and Family at Oklahoma Christian University for his encouraging words and suggestions. I am also grateful to John Hunter and other friends at College Press for their encouragement, design, printing, and distribution of this study. I am grateful to Dr. Carl Mitchell for guiding my wife and me through preparation for temperament analysis testing. I thank counselors Drs. Lynn McMillon and Kieth McKee for their encouragement of my efforts. Finally, I am thankful to my Lord for showing us through His Word how to have successful Christian marriages.

1

LOVE GOD ABOVE YOUR MATE – AND YOUR MATE AS YOURSELF

In this lesson:

- ▶ The danger of doing it "my way."
- ▶ God's rightful place in marriage
- ▶ Spiritual leadership in the family
- ▶ The Greatest Commandment and the "One Like It."
- ▶ God in mixed marriages

God's Word:

You shall have no other gods before me.

—Exodus 20:3

For this reason I kneel before the Father, from whom his whole family in heaven and on earth derives its name.

—Ephesians 3:14

"I did it my way," was Frank Sinatra's theme. He really did it his way, including being a partner in several failed marriages.

Our oldest son, Gerald, was and is an independent type. He longs to succeed on his own terms. Perhaps he got it from his father. His theme as a little youngster was, "My do it myself!" He sometimes got in over his head trying to do it himself before he was able.

Today's couples have been brainwashed into thinking that they can do marriage on their own terms and in their own way, each partner autonomous and largely independent of the other. Signs of this mentality are prenuptial agreements, separate checkbooks and separate professions. Some individual mates even go their own way in interests, hobbies, recreation, and vacations.

What they don't seem to realize is that "it takes two to tango." A marriage built on the sexual union of two free spirits may never be strong enough to last through the storms of life. When someone declares, "I'm tired of this marriage. I want out," he or she may really be saying, "I expected god (or goddess)-like status of my mate. Instead, he (or she) is merely human, warts and all."

> Today's couples have been brainwashed into thinking that they can do marriage on their own terms and in their own way,

GOD IS THE SENIOR PARTNER IN OUR MARRIAGE

In my book, *Marriage Is a Covenant, Not a Contract*, I reason that this relationship is entered into in the presence of God, with Him as the major party in it. He is the true head and senior partner of the marriage. If we have a proper relationship with Him, the chances are greater that the two lesser partners — husband and wife — will have a good relationship with each other.

> If we have a proper relationship with God, chances are greater of having a good relationship with each other.

Why is this? The couple has its priorities straight. Both husband and wife bow before their Maker, giving first allegiance to Him. As the Psalmist said, "It is he who made us, and we are his . . ." (Ps. 100:3).

Furthermore, our Lord says,". . . apart from me you can do nothing" (John 15:5).

If we can do nothing of any lasting significance without the Lord, the obvious implication is that we cannot truly succeed in marriage without Him.

JEALOUSY OVER A MATE'S DEDICATION TO THE LORD

Some marriage partners are jealous of their spouse who places the Lord first — resentful of the devotion and commitment given to God and His concerns. Especially those mates who are not Christians may see God (church) as a rival for the love of the believer and therefore fight against this perceived threat.

> In the realm of religious devotion, God has no rivals. He says clearly, "You shall have no other gods before me" (Exod. 20:3). God will tolerate no rivals. He must have all of the love and devotion and allegiance that one can give to a divine being. Such is the commitment the Christian has made to God.[1]

Of course, in the realm of marriage, each spouse is to have no rivals. They are to be totally committed to each other. It is a matter of priorities. Spiritually, however, it is God first, our spouses second, and ourselves third.

THE HUSBAND, FAMILY LEADER UNDER GOD

What does it mean to put the Lord first in our marital life?

First, the husband/father must take his place as the spiritual leader of the family. He is the acknowledged family head, but as Paul says in 1 Corinthians 11:3, ". . . the head of every man is Christ, and the head of the woman is man, and the head of Christ is God."

There is a clear hierarchy of authority and responsibility in Scripture which cannot be safely ignored if we are following God's order for our lives.

> Spiritually, it is God first, our spouses second, and ourselves third.

God must sit at the head of our table. His marital lieutenant is the husband, who has been delegated authority to serve as family leader. An early concept in the Bible is that of family priesthood. The father was to be the spiritual pacesetter or "point man" for his family.

> For I have chosen him [God speaking about Abraham], so that he will direct his children and his household after him to keep the way of the Lord by doing what is right and just (Gen. 18:18).

In his final instructions to Israel, one of Moses' admonitions was to parents, and especially to fathers,

> Love the Lord your God with all your heart and with all your soul and with all your strength. These commandments that I give you today are to be upon your hearts. Impress them on

your children. Talk about them when you sit at home and when you walk along the road, when you lie down and when you get up. Tie them as symbols on your hands and bind them on your foreheads. Write them on the doorframes of your houses and on your gates (Deut. 6:5-9).

I said recently to a young father who was neglecting his spiritual leadership, "Hey, it's Dad's place to be out front leading his family in spiritual exercises." How can this be true in our egalitarian society of today? Trust me. It's true because our Lord requires the household to have one marital and parental head.

DIRE CONSEQUENCES OF ABDICATING SPIRITUAL LEADERSHIP

According to God's design, the father, not the mother, is the head of the home. The mother cannot serve as spiritual leader in the family as well as the father. If she is the faithful one and he is not, this puts a nearly hopeless burden on her. She has to provide the spiritual impetus for the family, while he vegetates spiritually, abdicating to her his proper place in the family.

This role reversal may have dire consequences in the family's life. Sons often tend to rebel against religious activity, especially if the mother initiates it. Why? "If Dad doesn't think it's important, why should I?" Later on Dad may wonder what went wrong with the kids.

> "The need for more parental involvement, especially by fathers, is something many of us would rather not face."

Syndicated columnist Cal Thomas said this about the importance of the father's role in the family, based on research by a team of school teachers: ". . . mothers are frequently their children's heroes, but fathers, often described as emotionally or physically absent, are not. The need for more parental involvement, especially by fathers, is something many of us would rather not face."[2]

OUR ETERNAL TOYS

What else happens in a marriage in which God is removed from His throne? Toys! That's right, toys! We all have them — Monday Night Football, golf clubs, SUVs, rifles, fishing tackle, boats, the latest electronic gadgets — the list goes on and on. Yet Jesus tells us that we must sacrifice toys, and even our very selves, for His cause:

> Anyone who loves his father or mother more than me is not worthy of me; anyone who loves his son or daughter more than me is not worthy of me; and anyone who does not take his cross and follow me is not worthy of me. Whoever finds his life will lose it, and whoever loses his life for my sake will find it (Matt.10:37-39).

"Give up my toys? Not on your life!" So we worship our gadgets and drop our Creator to the role of an inferior deity or even a nondeity.

THE GREATEST COMMANDMENT

When Jesus was asked about the greatest commandment, He answered without hesitation, "Love the Lord your God with all your heart and with all your soul and with all your mind and with all your strength" (Mark 12:30).

"Love the Lord with all my heart? Wouldn't that leave no room for my mate and family?" Incredibly, it leaves more room. If we truly love the Lord pas-

> The more our hearts expand in love for our Lord, the more we will love others as well.

sionately, our heart grows to greater proportions. The love of God expands our being, so there is more room than ever for love, including love for our mates and offspring.

Let your mind drift back to the Dr. Seuss book, *How the Grinch Stole Christmas*. When the Grinch finally found Christmas, his tiny petrified heart expanded and expanded to reach out in love to the whole village he had mistreated earlier.

Precisely! The more our hearts expand in love for our Lord, the more we will love others as well. Could that be the reason why Jesus added a second commandment to the first, a second one of vital importance, one that goes to the very core of God's requirements for us: "Love your neighbor as yourself" (Mark 12:31)?

HOW DO WE PLACE GOD ON THE THRONE?

How do we go about placing God on the "throne" of our heart? We reorganize our priorities. We drop out of our lives everything that impedes us from loving Him unconditionally. Do yourself a favor. Love God with all your heart, soul, mind, and strength, and you will find you have greater love for your spouse and family. His life will rub off on you, and the blessings will flow over you and into your home.

Of course, your spouse must have the same desire to place God first in his or her life. That may be a difficult barrier to your spiritual life, but one which can be overcome. In speaking to

Christians married to non-Christians, Paul asked, "How do you know, wife, whether you will save your husband?

> Your spouse should have the same desire to place God first.

Or, how do you know, husband, whether you will save your wife?" (1 Cor. 7:16).

One of our major purposes in life as Christians is to introduce others to the Savior, beginning with our own household. If you are married to someone who has an entirely different view of God and church than you, great patience and a stellar example are called for. However, even if you cannot influence your mate to become a Christian, you must still be faithful to the Lord and must continue to set a consistent example of loving care to your family.

Parting Proverb:
Keep God at the head of your table, house, family, and life.

NOTES

1. Jack Harriman, minister of the Center Street Church of Christ, Fayetteville, Arkansas, Sept. 5, 1999.

2. Cal Thomas, *The Daily Oklahoman*, 17 Oct. 1999.

Reflecting on Lesson One

1. Can any of us safely live our life our way? If not, why?

2. What do you think has contributed to the sense of autonomy between marriage partners?

3. Why is a marriage built on sexual union alone subject to later problems?

4. Discuss some dangers inherent in a marriage between a believer and an unbeliever.

5. Why must the Lord be the Senior Partner in a marriage and home?

6. What is the biblical place of the husband/father in a home? To whom does he answer in God's scheme of things? What is the scriptural hierarchy designed by God for marriage?

7. What obligations do parents have toward their children?

8. What are the consequences of abdicating our proper role in marriage and the family?

9. When God is removed from His throne, what do families often substitute for Him? How do we go about placing the Lord on the throne of our hearts and homes?

Consider this:

How would you like it if your spouse kept a picture on the nightstand of someone he/she used to date? Do you think God likes it any better when we continue to place other things in our lives ahead of Him? Before reading lesson two think about how you would deal with such unfaithfulness if you were God.

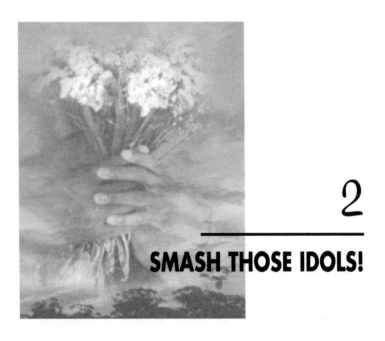

2

SMASH THOSE IDOLS!

In this lesson:
- ▶ Defining idolatry
- ▶ Listing some idols
- ▶ Fallen idols
- ▶ Getting rid of idols

God's Word:
You shall not make for yourself an idol . . .
Exod. 20:4

For everything in the world — the cravings of sinful man,
the lust of his eyes and the boasting of what he has and does —
comes not from the Father but from the world.
—1 John 2:16

Put to death, therefore, whatever belongs to your earthly nature: sexual immorality, impurity, lust, evil desires and greed, which is idolatry.
—Colossians 3:5

"Who, me? I'm certainly not an idolater. Look in my home. You'll find no prayer niches, lit candles, incense, or images."

Not an idolater? Anything you place above God or even in competition with Him becomes your idol.

What is it? Money? Investments? That "hog" in your driveway? Your RV? Position? Prestige? Your ball team? Your secretary? Even your mate? We have all seen people whose idol is their favorite football team, actor, singer, TV personality, sports card collection, house, clothes, classic car, beer, cigarettes, drugs, pornography, Internet chat rooms, profession, hunting, fishing, bridge . . . . I know men who go into a fit of depression if a stormy Saturday keeps them off the golf course.

> Anything you place above God or even in competition with Him becomes your idol.

IDOLIZING OTHER PEOPLE

Some have even idolized religious leaders. While we were living in Brazil the Pope visited our city. He was actually worshiped by many in the crowds that came out to see and hear him, as they chanted, "The Pope is our God! The Pope is our God!" Some here in the U.S. have elevated healers or charismatic televangelists to almost godlike status. However, with the fall of several of these "superapostles," perhaps the gullibility of their audience has decreased a little.

Some people have idolized their mate, girl friend, or boy friend. Then, when they discover that their dream person is not perfect after all, their love changes to disappointment or even hatred. One of King David's sons, Amnon, had a severe case of lovesickness for his half sister, Tamar, until he allowed his passion to possess him, becoming a rapist. Then his avowed "love" turned quickly into hatred (2 Sam. 13).

There is no perfect person. Some may have gorgeous hair, a great figure, an inventive mind, or an iron build, but I can guarantee that they have feet of clay, or at least a toe or two of clay. Abraham was lauded by God for his faith, yet twice he lied, risking his wife's future to save his own skin. David, the great psalmist, warrior, and king — a man after God's own heart — committed adultery and murder. "God, be merciful to me, a sinner," should be our daily prayer, for we all sin and fall far short of God's glory (Rom. 3:23).

A certain young ruler had it all — power, position, possessions, and youth. He was drawn to Jesus and expressed a sincere desire to follow Him. The Lord had compassion for him, but saw that the young man had an idol — his possessions. When he was told to get rid of that one "god" that kept him from the one true God, he walked away downcast. He just couldn't smash that idol!

IDOLS IN MY OWN LIFE

What are some idols I have battled? I've never had wealth nor expensive possessions. Except for a VW van our sponsoring church furnished for us on the mission field, I have never owned a "0"-mile car. Normally the cars I have owned have been several years old when they came into my hands. I have never lived in a new house; most have been older and rented. I don't own a set of golf clubs. I can take football or leave it. I have no interest in hunting. I like to fish, but seldom go fishing and have no fishing gear.

Then what drives me? A desire to be a truly great and recognized artist, author, and songwriter. Earlier in my life I longed to be a gifted speaker, singer, and athlete. I can speak adequately, can sing moderately well, and have won my share of distance races until age took its toll. Age, however, has also taught me that I will never be a Norman Rockwell, a Placido Domingo, a Michael Jordan, or a male counterpart of hymn writer Fanny Crosby. At this point, I have no delusions about ever being a company president or a great public figure.

How many idols have you brought into your marriage and home?

So be it! These idols in my life have been hammered down with difficulty and may not be fully destroyed yet.

YOU AND YOUR IDOLS

And you? How many idols have you brought into your marriage and home? God knows. Are you honest enough with Him and yourself to be your own iconoclast, facing up to and destroying your idols with God's help? I have been in many countries where images are visible everywhere. Some are beautiful and some are grotesque. In a museum in Brazil I noticed that many small images in the collection were missing arms, legs, and even heads. I asked an attendant about this. He explained, "These were household saints in colonial days. When the saint didn't grant a devotee's wish, the saint was punished. An arm, leg, or even head was broken off and the image was turned toward the wall."

How silly! We would never do something like that. Or would we? Have you ever seen a husband or wife who had put the mate on a pedestal — until age, illness, or some other setback appeared. Down from the pedestal the person fell. The result? His or her mate soon sought someone else to idolize.

Of course, we must love our spouse and family, but that love can never be all-consuming to the point where God is dethroned. He must have first place in our marriage, home, and life. If we ever face a choice between God and our spouse, Heaven forbid, our Lord must be glorified at all costs.

> Love of spouse and family can never be all-consuming to the point where God is dethroned.

YANK UP THOSE IDOLS

Now, what about those idols in our lives? They must be yanked up and destroyed as weeds from a garden. They may go deeply into our soul and even our home. In some parts of the country we know about Johnson grass. I discovered one summer, when attempting to get rid of a patch of that pesky grass, that its roots went down three feet or more. Moreover, If even one root segment was left, it would sprout back up with a vengeance. Likewise, any idol left on its pedestal in our heart will take over our allegiance again.

A Brazilian language teacher, who was a practicing Catholic, married her student, an American missionary. When she decided to become a Christian, she wanted to make a total break with her religious past. Carrying her images, rosaries, pictures, and other paraphernalia of her former faith out of her home, she destroyed

> Any idol left on its pedestal in our heart will take over our allegiance again.

them. This is exactly what we must do with our own personal idols. It doesn't matter whether those images are physical icons or images of power, prestige, money, sports, or some individual. They must be yanked out of our hearts and never allowed to grow back.

Do we really want a pure life and holy marriage? Then we must quit forming and worshiping our own little idols. Your wife would not like to see a photo of your former fiancée or your secretary on your desk at work. Nor does our Lord put up with our competing "gods." He is the Lord; there is no other. If He is not our only object of worship, we will eventually destroy ourselves, our mates, and our families in an idolatrous quest for temporal things or social power.

Parting Proverb:
God doesn't put up with competition, nor does your mate.

Reflecting on Lesson Two

1. Explain how anything you place above God or in competition with Him is idolatry.

2. What is the danger in idolizing any human being?

3. What was the "idol" the rich young ruler worshiped?

4. What are some idols to which you have fallen? What are some you have overcome?

5. Why must our love never be all-consuming for anyone but God?

6. Why is it necessary to smash all of our idols in order to follow God?

7. How can our idolatry undermine our personal and marital life?

8. What do the Scriptures mean when they say that we should love the Lord our God with all of our heart, soul, mind, and strength?

9. If we love the Lord in this way, how can we also love our mate and family?

Consider this:

In preparing for lesson three think about what it means to misuse God's name (or take it in vain, as the older versions put it). Since our spouses are to be next in our affections and honor after God, does your speech reflect that high position? How do you talk about your spouse to others? Do the things you say to your spouse build up or tear down? Keep tabs on your speech this week and see what it reveals.

3

DON'T BADMOUTH YOUR MATE

In this lesson:
▶ The ill effects of criticism
▶ The power of positive reinforcement
▶ Sweetening the pill of correction

God's Word:

You will not misuse the name of the Lord your God.

—Exodus 20:7

Do not let any unwholesome talk come out of your mouths, but only what is helpful for building others up according to their needs.

—Ephesians 4:29

Have you ever known a husband or wife who incessantly criticized his or her mate, even in public? This vicious practice seems to be nearly epidemic. Some people seem to have a personal devil which prods them into constantly criticizing their spouse, either seriously or in jest.

NEGATIVE INPUT IS DESTRUCTIVE

Rather than improving the other person through nagging and belittling, the reverse is generally true. The very things with which the mate is charged can become self-fulfilling. For instance, if he is called a no-good, filthy pig often enough, the chances are that he will become just that.

> Some people seem to have a personal devil which prods them into constantly criticizing their spouses.

Pat Summitt is the head coach of Tennessee's Lady Volunteers basketball team. Her team has won three recent national titles, but at a price. The team had lost a game that it should have won. Summitt criticized one of her players so severely that the girl couldn't sleep that night. She called her coach the next morning and said, "I need some encouragement. I don't need to be ridden all the time and just lashed out at . . . I'm not responding to that."[1] This same kind of thing happened to me in college track. Instead of encouraging me, my coach would only say, "You can do better than that." His unsupportive response caused me to believe that I probably couldn't do better.

In sharp contrast, in Brazil I helped organize a runner's club and ran frequently in competition. A top distance runner and coach took me under his wing and made sure I felt good about myself and my progress. He spread the word around that I was the best in the 5- or 10-K run for my age group. Because he believed in me, I was determined not to let him down.

Do you see the difference between these two approaches to coaching? One discourages; the other builds up. The same differences can exist in marriage. We have a choice. We can either build up our spouse, or we can tear him or her down. Constant negativism is like a dripping faucet. Eventually it will drive our marriage partner to distraction and even retaliation.

> We can either build up our spouse, or we can tear him or her down.

NAGGING MATES AND DRIPPING FAUCETS

Nothing is much more discouraging than a nagging wife. The wise man, Solomon, said it well, and he was an authority. He had a palace full of wives.

> Better to live on a corner of the roof than share a house with a quarrelsome wife (Prov. 21:9).

The other side of the coin is also true. A constantly complaining and objecting husband can drive his wife to refuse sex, strike back, run away, or even divorce him.

One positive exercise for mates who are faultfinders is to ask them to list ten things they like about their partner. In some cases it might stretch their mind to the breaking point to come up with ten such traits, but surely they can list some. If they will dwell on these, the negative points may begin to recede.

We know we are not to take the Lord's name in vain, nor are we to take our marriage partner's name in vain. This calls for us to refuse to curse him or her, slander, injure with our tongue, undermine, gossip, or engage in any other form of verbal or mental abuse, not to mention physical abuse.

Shouting matches, harsh arguments, tossing around barbed words — such behavior has no place in our marital relations. Of course, this includes talking negatively about our mate to others, in our partner's presence or not. Even if done in jest, such words can do great damage. One area of special sensitivity is that of appearance. Both genders are touchy in this area and may even be very uncomfortable about their weight or appearance. This whole subject is a veritable field of land mines. Even if the mate asks our opinion about his or her weight or other characteristics, we need to walk very carefully and speak only out of love and concern for the other's well being.

> Even if done in jest, disparaging descriptions can do great damage.

APPLYING POSITIVE REINFORCEMENT

In place of negative behavior, it is much wiser and more Christlike to build up our partner with positive reinforcement. If we want to see our mate glow, praise him or her in public and, of course, in private as well.

Women, tell your man that he has a great body and is a wonderful lover. Watch him try to measure up to this image and perform even better. Tell him how much you appreciate his leadership of the family, his caring for the yard, his helping with the housework and children, his care for his family, and his professional skills.

Men, compliment your wives on their attractiveness, dress, care of the home, sexual ability, dedication, commitment to the

> Compliments must have some real meat to them, and not just baloney.

children, endearing personality, and work ethic. In all of this mean it. If it is baloney we are dishing out, it is still baloney. Compliments must have some meat to them.

BATHING UNPLEASANT MATTERS IN OIL OF PRAISE AND SINCERITY

If we must bring up something unpleasant, we need to make certain it is bathed in the oil of praise and loving sincerity. Even in dealing with a corrupted Corinthian church, Paul prefaced his correction with praise. In addressing the seven churches of Asia, Jesus had some words of encouragement before pointing out their errors (Rev. 2 and 3).

The old adage is true: You can attract more bees with honey than with vinegar. Scripture bears this out. Paul gave some clear instructions to both husband and wife about their care for each other:

> Wives, submit to your husbands as to the Lord. For the husband is the head of the wife as Christ is the head of the church . . . Now as the church submits to Christ, so also wives should submit to their husbands in everything.
> Husbands, love your wives, just as Christ loved the church and gave himself up for her . . . each one of you also must love his wife as he loves himself, and the wife must respect her husband (Eph. 5:22-33).

So we must be kind, gentle, and considerate toward each other. This is the Lord's will for us. Do you suppose that such behavior might make marriage much more interesting? Do you suppose it might cut way down on the likelihood of separation and divorce?

Parting Proverb:
If your mouth is full of acid, get rid of it and ask God to heal your mouth and your heart.

NOTES

1 *Reader's Digest*, Feb. 2000, p. 56.

Reflecting on Lesson Three

1. What is the predictable consequence of constantly belittling and criticizing your mate?

2. Why is it better to affirm your mate than to criticize him or her?

3. What effect can a complaining and objecting mate have on marital (including sexual) relations?

4. Why are our weight and appearance such sensitive areas for others to criticize?

5. Suggest some ways in which we can give positive reinforcement to the good traits of our mate.

6. What should be our motivation for compliments?

7. If we must bring up something negative, how should we clothe it?

8. What can kindness, gentleness, and consideration do for marriage?

9. How can you begin to put these traits to work in your marriage?

Consider this:

Before reading lesson four, answer the following questions: How do you and your spouse recognize special days such as anniversaries, birthdays, Mother's and Father's Day, etc.? Have you ever talked about this? Is it possible that one mate is dissatisfied with the attention given to special occasions? What could you change to make lasting memories of some of these days?

4

HONOR YOUR MATE'S SPECIAL DAYS

In this lesson:
- ▶ The Christian's health and social advantages
- ▶ Christian love in action
- ▶ Nurturing love with special attention
- ▶ Taking time for God and each other

God's Word:

Remember the Sabbath day by keeping it holy.

—Exodus 20:8

Give everyone what you owe him . . . if honor, then honor. Let no debt remain outstanding, except the continuing debt to love one another . . . .

—Romans 13:7-8

A 1999 survey by Duke University revealed that people who actively participate in a church on the whole have better health and live longer than those who don't.

> People who actively participate in a church have better health and live longer than those who don't.

"Why is this?" asked news anchors. They concluded that most churchgoers lead a clean life, have a strong support base in fellow church members, a reason for living, and a hope beyond their physical life.

CHRISTIANS REALLY DO HAVE ADVANTAGES

This makes sense. Dedicated Christians do have all of the above advantages. Most are nonsmokers. They do not engage in any kind of dissipation. They know they have the prayers and support of other Christians. They certainly have a strong faith in the Lord's forgiveness and saving power for eternity. They can face serious illness and death in trust, looking to Jesus and their faith in the resurrection (1 Thess. 4:14; Heb. 12:2).

I remember when I was flat on my back with polio just prior to the invention of the vaccine. I had been staff artist for a church publishing plant — my first job out of college. After I had been five years with the plant, the owner had serious personal difficulties, so I left, going to work for a commercial printer.

Then tragedy struck and I was down for months. The doctor and nurse gave themselves to my care, staying all night by my bed. I remember the doctor's words to my precious wife, Margie, that I might never walk again. I said to myself, "I'll show you. I'll not only walk again, but I'll run." Several dozen medals, trophies, and ribbons from distance races in more recent years attest to my resolve.

But enough of that. While I was ill, Margie worked swing shift at a meat packing plant to keep a roof over our heads. She could even bring home meat scraps. She wasn't the only provider, however. Every week a pickup truck came to our door with food and other necessities contributed by the small congregation where I had been preaching part-time. Talk about a support base! The members prayed and worked to save our little family from starvation and even worse — indifference.

CHRISTIANS RALLY TO CRISES

We have seen this over and over. Give Christians a real need or crisis and watch them rally to it. In recent years earthquakes, tornadoes, hurricanes, floods, fires, bombings, war, and other disasters have devastated our world time and time again. Without fail believers come to the aid of victims, generally remaining and serving there much longer than public service organizations or government agencies. Yes, we are a caring people, and this is a great blessing both for us and the recipients of our care.

Beyond all of this, we have a real hope — hope for the con-

> Give Christians a real need or crisis and watch them rally to it.

stant presence of Jesus' Spirit, the continuing forgiveness of sins through His blood, His intercession for us on a daily basis, His saving and reassuring Word, the fact of resurrection, and a secure future with our Lord in Heaven.

Because of His great love and provision for us, we know we are important to Him. As Dr. M. Scott Peck says,

It matters whether we take that drink. It matters whether we slap our child. It matters whether we cheat on our income tax. It matters when we risk telling the truth. It matters when we go out of our way to help another. The day-to-day state of our soul matters. It matters because we are loved.[1]

We are loved by our Lord, by Christians in our midst, and by our spouse. At least we hope our mate loves us, even as unlovable as we may be at times. Unconditional love is all-important. Imagine what it would be like if God's love were conditional, depending on our situation at the moment. And

Unconditional love is all-important.

our marital love? Is it unconditional or does it ebb and flow, depending on the vagaries of the moment? It too must be unconditional, warts and all.

LOVE MUST BE NURTURED

Yet, our marital love needs to be nurtured. It needs to be reinforced. We can never afford to ignore times that are important to our mate or to both of us as a couple — anniversaries, birthdays, Mother's Day, Father's Day, Thanksgiving, Christmas, vacation times, Friday nights out, etc. One time I made the gross error of overlooking Mother's Day. When my loving wife noted that I had not even given her a card, I countered with the lame excuse that, after all, she was not my mother. Not a good answer! Since then I have never failed to honor her on Mother's Day.

I've done much better about wedding anniversaries. Especially in the past quarter century or more we have arranged for a couple of days away from home, perhaps to the mountains, to a resort, or just to a nearby bed-and-breakfast to celebrate our anniversary. We renew our love and commitment to each other during those special hours away. As I wrote this, we were on a cruise in the Aegean Sea to celebrate our Golden Wedding Anniversary. This, of course, was with the help of many family members and friends. How can we ever top that as an anniversary get-away?

SLOW DOWN AND SMELL THE FLOWERS

Not only these special days, but also others are important if we are to remember our Lord, our partner, and our family. Some people claim they are too busy for worship or church activity, too busy for family, and too busy for a vacation together. If so, they are too busy. It is important to "slow down and smell the flowers." And this from a chronic workaholic, who really is trying to slow down.

Dr. Peck, whom I quoted earlier in this chapter, takes two hours a day for Bible reading, prayer, and meditation. Martin Luther is said to have devoted four hours a day to such spiritual exercises. When asked how he could accomplish this since he had so much to do, he answered, "I couldn't do the other if I didn't do this."[2] As the old saying goes, "we're too soon old and too late smart" to keep our true priorities intact.

Deliberately taking time for the Lord, spouse, and family pays rich dividends. If

> If you are too busy for worship or church activity — or too busy to have special times for your family — you are too busy.

we are thinking "Gospel of Prosperity," that's not what I mean. We are not promised an unending life of wealth, happiness, and freedom from pain. Jesus said that we must leave all to follow Him. He reminded us that in this world we would have tribulation, but also that in Him our joy is complete.

Our joy in marriage can also be complete by walking together in our Lord's steps, remembering His day each week, and remembering all of the special days of our mate and family. We may never have much of this world's goods, but we will be rich toward God and toward each other as husband and wife.

You busy husband, take time to converse with your wife and really listen to her. That might give her a heart attack, but try it anyway. And you harried wives, with a full van and empty heart, find a way to continually remember your Lord and your mate.

Parting Proverb:

Be sneaky if you have to, but surprise your mate with a memorable anniversary and birthday. It may cost, but it's guaranteed to pay.

NOTES

1. M. Scott Peck, Jr., *The Road Less Traveled and Beyond* (Collingsdale, PA: Dianna, 1999), 56.

2. See Kenneth Scott Latourette, *A History of Christianity* (New York: Harper & Row, 1975).

Reflecting on Lesson Four

1. What was concluded from a Duke University survey about Christians having better health and a longer life than non-Christians?

2. What value does a strong support base have for Christians?

3. Why can a Christian face serious illness and death calmly?

4. What is the usual response of Christians to a disaster or crisis?

5. How does our Lord show His love for us?

6. Why does it matter how we behave toward our mates and others?

7. Why is it necessary for love to be nurtured?

8. Why is it important to slow down and smell the flowers?

9. Suggest how you and your mate can learn better to really communicate in a loving way.

Consider this:

One of the difficult lessons for parents these days is to teach children respect in a self-centered society that elevates independence and self-determination. Before the next lesson, evaluate how you model respect for elders. Do you show less respect for your in-laws than for other adults? Is your stated respect for your parents proven by your actions? As they learn from you, will your children show you respect in your old age and expect the same from their spouses?

5

ENJOY YOUR PARENTS AND EACH OTHER

In this lesson:

- ▶ Respecting your elders
- ▶ Outward signs of respect
- ▶ Practicing respect
- ▶ Deserving respect

God's Word:

*Honor your father and your mother, so that you may live long
in the land the Lord your God is giving you.*

—Exodus 20:12

*Do not rebuke an older man harshly, but exhort him as if
he were your father. Treat younger men as brothers,
older women as mothers, and younger women as sisters.*

—1 Timothy 5:1-2

Mother-in-law jokes abound, but they are out of place in God's scheme of things. We are to honor our parents and, by extension, our mate's parents. In so doing we will give them a happier life and we, too, will have both a more satisfying and longer life.

How do we go about honoring our parents? Well, we may be thirty or forty

> We are to honor our parents and, by extension, our mate's parents.

or more, but we still are not too far along in years to respect them, their views and wishes. Who knows? Their age and experience may have taught them lessons that we can learn without falling into the traps that awaited them on every side.

In our age of disregard for the elderly, all too often we seem to feel that they know nothing worthwhile. They may not know the latest technology, but they do know life, and that is a lesson learned only through decades of often painful experience. It is a strange paradox that we have children when we have had little experience yet with life and even less with bringing up offspring. By the time we know something in these areas, we are too old to bear more children.

HOW DO WE HONOR OUR PARENTS?

We live at a time when there is no longer any respect for older people. In fact, they are almost considered "throw-aways." We're to a degree like some Eskimo tribes. When a tribal patriarch or matriarch can no longer carry his or her share of the work, that person is placed on an ice drift to die of exposure at sea. We're not so cruel as to do that. We just hide our elderly away or decide to pull the plug on their life-support system.

My own mother spent her last years in intensive care because she was beyond our help. The day we had to place her in a nursing home was traumatic for us. Rationally, we knew we could no longer care for her, but emotionally, it seemed to us like betraying her.

There are cases in which we are forced to relinquish our personal care for our parents, but we can still visit, love, and minister to them until the end. My wife Margie's mother is 91 and lives, by her own choice, in her own tiny apartment near us. Margie sees to her laundry, shopping, doctor's visits, and other needs. Margie still works, but also devotes attention to her mother several times a week, as tiring as that is.

> Some of the best counseling I ever got growing up was from my mother's father.

In our society, unlike some others, elderly parents cannot dictate to their grown children. Perhaps not, but they may have excellent advice and are certainly due respect, love, and attention. If respect for the elderly is built into the home training of children, parents will likely receive respect from them in turn.

By extension, our respect for parents should include grandparents and older aunts and uncles as well. Some of the best counseling I ever got growing up was from my mother's father, a church elder and a wise and gentle man.

How do we go about honoring our collective parents? By showing respect for them in what we say and do. By showing them loving care, not constant meddling. We recently watched a man cruising with us on the Aegean. He was most attentive to an elderly woman traveling with him and his wife. We asked him if she was his mother. He answered, "No, she's my surrogate mother." Even more remarkable!

RESPECT INSTILLED INTO CHILDREN

This whole mindset of respect for those who are older, and especially parents, must be instilled into children, many of whom have the unfortunate tendency to be young tyrants.

To illustrate, while we lived in Brazil, I was preaching one Sunday morning in a small church which met in a rented residence. A side door was open, and I saw a young mother outside trying to reason with her rambunctious son, who was four or five years of age. He, in turn, kicked her several times. I had it, stopped preaching, went out, and grabbed him, saying, "If I ever see you kick your mother again, I will shake you until your teeth rattle." He didn't know if I would really do that, but never again in my presence did he abuse his mother.

We must teach youngsters to respect all older people and especially their own parents. One teenage boy I know always greets me at church services in a polite manner, using "Sir." His respect is rare, indeed. Obviously, he learned something important from his parents. (Some of our own children tried to talk back to us at their own risk, but one of them was different. He never talked back; he just slammed a door to show his displeasure at us and that got him into trouble!) Those who are young par-

> Not only must we talk about respect, we must practice it.

ents will do well to instill this kind of deference for those older than they.

To Instill Respect, Practice It

Not only must we talk about respect, we must practice it. We must not only tell; we must show. By giving our seat on a crowded bus to an elderly person, by showing great regard for our own parents, and by other acts of respect, we set a positive example for our children.

In this process of example-setting, we parents must show care and tenderness for each other. Verbal and physical abuse teach only abusive behavior to our kids. Even when we badmouth other adults about us, gossip about them, or fail to show loving regard for them, and especially in the church, we teach our children disregard for adults.

How can children learn respect when they hear us crucify others with our tongues, cheat others, or lie to others? How can they learn respect unless we respect them as people? A better, kinder, more respectful world really does begin with us.

> How can children learn respect when they hear us crucify others with our tongues.

To Be Honored, Be Honorable

To be honored, of course, we must be honorable. It is difficult to show consideration for unlovely people, yet Jesus did it. He was often seen in the company of cheating tax collectors, prostitutes, and other "low life." As far as the powerful of Jesus' time were concerned, these were hopeless prodigals unworthy of their attention. Our Lord, however, treated them with kindness, and they responded penitently: "Lord, I believe. Help my unbelief." Or, "Depart from me, Lord, for I am a sinful man."

Since we are all sinners, let us regard others, especially our parents, grandparents, and spouses with honor and patience, and they will eventually respond in kind.

Parting Proverb:

Treat your mother-in-law with kindness and she may even come to think you're worthy of her child.

Reflecting on Lesson Five

1. What do the Scriptures say about honoring parents and other elderly people?

2. Why has our present society lost its sense of respect for the elderly?

3. Why is it important to instill into our children respect for parents, grandparents, and other older people?

4. How can we go about honoring our parents and parents-in-law?

5. What part does our example play in teaching respect for others?

6. Why is it important to be honorable?

7. How can we best show consideration for people who are unlovely and unlovable?

8. Why should we treat others, and especially aging parents, with patience?

9. Explain why respect and honor must begin in the home.

Consider this:

Jesus made it clear that there are many ways to murder. Killing the spirit of a person is as deadly as killling their body — even more so. Are you your brother's keeper? You do have a responsibility to nurture the spirit of those around you, particularly those closest to you. Delve into the depths of these ideas before starting on lesson six.

6

DON'T EVEN THINK ABOUT MURDERING YOUR MATE

In this lesson:

▶ How to murder without a murder charge
▶ Different ways to kill love

God's Word:
You shall not murder.
—Exodus 20:13

You have heard that it was said to the people long ago, "Do not murder, and anyone who murders will be subject to judgment." But I tell you that anyone who is angry with his brother will be subject to judgment.
—Matthew 5:21-22

The O.J. Simpson case was a real shocker, and so was the long, convoluted trial that brought a questionable innocent verdict for him. So the case goes on unsolved. We see all of the gory details on TV about men and women killing their mates, parents, or children. We learn, to our dismay, about children gunning down their own family members.

If such extreme scenarios don't actually occur, the next steps below it do — harshness, abuse, neglect, marital unfaithfulness, and a general disrespect for life.

William Murcheson notes on this that when we take, extinguish, or foreclose that which our ancestors understood only to be in the hands of God, we find our feet on a slippery slope and downward we coast to an animal level of existence.[1]

HATRED AMOUNTS TO MURDER

"You shall not kill" has been one of God's commands for a long, long time. Jesus expanded on it to declare that if we even hate another person, we have already killed that individual in our heart.

Why such a seemingly harsh judgment on our motives? Scientists who subscribe to evolution declare that life is a mere accident, that we are nothing more than evolved animals. So we act like animals, hating and killing with little compunction or remorse. If we believe we originally came from slime, we eventually become slime.

> There are many ways to kill besides using a weapon to end a life.

You may object at this point, arguing, "'You shall not kill' excludes me. In no way would I actually kill anyone, even in a flash of anger."

Perhaps not, but there are many ways to kill besides using poison, a knife, gun, or some other weapon to end a life. Here are some:

HOW WE KILL WITHOUT A WEAPON

Selfishness

The person who is wrapped up in self makes a very small package. When selfishness rules our life, everything we do is tainted by it. My mother taught my brother and me to give in to our little sister with the order, "Ladies first." The day when she grabbed some candy and said, "Me first," was the day when Mother modified her method. Some, though, never grow out of the "me first" syndrome. Witness the "road rage" that goes on today. The perpetrators of road rage appear to believe they have every right to be first, and no one else should infringe on that right. Such a mentality can destroy the very fabric of marriage because it places self on the throne and makes the mate a mere servant.

Hatred

Spite for our mate, family, relatives, or in-laws is a form of murder — an ever-so-slow poison that consumes us and destroys those close to us. Hatred can be masked in various ways. What are some of these? It can be masked as insincere praise, lying, deceiving and hurtful words, lack of consideration, and selfishness.

> Hatred can be masked in various ways.

Nagging

Nagging is that constant drip-drip of attempting to force one's mate or family into conformity. The wise man said, "It is better to live on a corner of the roof than share a house with a quarrelsome wife" (Prov. 21:9). Naggers may successfully kill the spirit of others. They may conform, true, but not voluntarily, and may end up resenting and hating the nagger.

> Naggers may successfully kill the spirit of others.

Criticizing

Criticism is a process of dismantling the spirit and self-esteem of others. It may take the form of direct reproof or public complaining in the presence or absence of the other person. If a mate or offspring is constantly told that he or she is worthless, unloved, stupid, or ugly, that person may eventually fulfill the criticism, at least in attitude.

Abuse

Abuse can be physical or verbal. Physical abuse may not kill the body, but it certainly kills the spirit of the mate. In order to keep the family together, or perhaps to feed a complex of codependency, the mistreated mate may stay for many years with the abuser, putting up with near-murder. By the way, either mate can be a physical or verbal abuser.

Don't Even Think about Murdering Your Mate

Lying and Deceit

Marriages must be built on honesty. This does not mean insensitive blurting out of truth, but tactful use of it. It means being transparent, not deceitful. We can kill our mate, little by little, just through a lying or withholding tongue.

Willful Neglect or Indifference

This too is a form of murder, for love is eventually killed by indifference. The man who boasts that he feels no need to buy gifts for his wife, even on her birthday, their anniversary, or Mother's Day is a love-murderer. She may say that she doesn't really need a gift, but in reality

> Love is eventually killed by indifference.

she longs for one. That man is foolish who doesn't have a clue as to how to read her true feelings. And she, in turn, is foolish if she ignores her husband's special days or other opportunities to buy something for him or give him moral support.

Dr. Joe Harding tells about a man who finally decided to ask his boss for a raise. He told his wife what he was going to do. All day long he was stressed out, but finally raked up the courage to approach his employer. To his delight, the boss agreed to a raise.

The man arrived home to a table set with their best china. His wife had prepared a festive meal. Finding her in the kitchen, he told her the good news. They kissed and then sat down to a wonderful meal. Next to his plate he found a beautiful note. It read: "Congratulations, darling! I knew you'd get the raise! These things will tell you how much I love you."

On the way to the kitchen to get the dessert he noticed a sec-

Ten Commandments for Couples

ond card that had fallen out of her pocket. It read: "Don't worry about not getting the raise! You deserve it anyway! These things will tell you how much I love you." Total acceptance and total moral support — this is a goal toward which we work as couples.[2]

Withholding Sex

This is another way to murder the spirit of one's marriage partner. Unless there is serious illness or, as Paul said in 1 Corinthians 7, a mutually-determined period of abstention for the purpose of fasting and prayer, then we have no right to rob our mate of his or her sexual due.

Withholding sex may be done out of ulterior motives — revenge, blackmail, or disinterest. "He did me dirt, so he can just sleep on the couch." "If I give him sex, maybe I can hold onto him." Or, "Oh, go ahead and do it. I could care less" — these are signs of marital sickness. Whatever the reason behind it, prolonged sexual abstinence can easily lead to infidelity or at least serious temptation.

> Prolonged sexual abstinence can easily lead to infidelity.

Manipulation

We have just discussed sex for purposes of blackmail. Could it also be a means of manipulating our mate — granting sex in exchange for some favor? Sounds a bit like legal prostitution, doesn't it? Manipulation can be used to maneuver our mate into a purchase about which he or she has doubts or participating in an event that he or she really doesn't enjoy.

Failure to Share in Domestic Responsibilities or Finances

I have heard many a wife say that their husbands could not even boil an egg, that they never did any housework, or that they did not help care for or discipline the kids. Especially if both work outside the home, then both must share in domestic tasks. For harmony in the home, they must also share in financial matters. A husband who has always "protected" his wife from family business or financial matters has not prepared her for life after his death, in case he predeceases her. Marriage — the good, the bad, and the ugly — must be a shared experience. We must protect our mate but not overprotect him or her. It is unfair to conceal important matters from our spouse.

> Marriage — the good, the bad, and the ugly — must be a shared experience.

General Neglect

Habitual couch potatoes, golf players, card sharks, gamblers, or bar denizens, beware! You may be killing your marriage through neglect. During our years in Brazil we saw much of this. In the Brazilian culture men assume that they have every right to spend their evenings at the local bar, leaving their mate at home to corral the kids and put them to bed. We may not spend most of our evenings with the "boys," but still spend far too much time away from family. We work long hours, travel, sign up for all the bowling leagues, and otherwise tie up our evenings and weekends. You workaholics, habitually enslaving yourselves to your profession, and you slaves to your hobbies, also beware! You may be married to your pastime, rather than to your spouse.

These ways of behaving are not murder, in a legal sense, but they are in an emotional and spiritual sense. God still warns us, "You shall not murder."

The Point System in Marriage

In the world of romance, one single rule applies: Make the woman happy! Do something she likes and you get points. Do something she dislikes and points are subtracted. You don't get any points for doing something she expects. Sorry, that's the way the game is played.

> You don't get any points for merely doing something your spouse expects.

Here is the guide to a point system that came via e-mail from an unknown source:

Simple Duties:

You make the bed	+1
You make the bed, but forget to add the decorative pillows	0
You throw the bedspread over rumpled sheets	-1
You leave the toilet seat up	-5
You replace the toilet-paper roll when it's empty	0
You check out a suspicious noise at night	0
You check out a suspicious noise & it's nothing	0
You check out a suspicious noise and it's something	+5
You pummel it with a six iron	+10
It's her pet	-10

Social Engagements:

You stay by her side the entire party	0

You stay by her side for a while, then leave to chat with a college buddy	-2
Named Tiffany	-4

Her Birthday:

You take her out to dinner	0
You take her out to dinner and it's not a sports bar	+1
Okay, it is a sports bar	-2
And it's all-you-can-eat night	-3
It's a sports bar, it's all-you-can-eat night and your face is painted the colors of your favorite team	-10

A Night Out:

You take her to a movie	+2
You take her to a movie she likes	+4
You take her to a movie you hate	+6
You take her to a movie you like	-2
It's called Death Cop III	-3

Your Physique:

You develop a noticeable potbelly	-15
You develop a noticeable potbelly and exercise to get rid of it	+10
You develop a noticeable potbelly and resort to loose jeans and baggy Hawaiian shirts	-30
You say, "It doesn't matter, you have one too."	-800

The Big Question: She asks, "Do I look fat?"

You hesitate in responding	-10
You reply, "Where?"	-35
Any other response	-20

(Sorry, there's no way out of this one without a loss of points.)

Communication:

> When she wants to talk about a problem, you listen, displaying
> what looks like a concerned expression   0
>
> When she wants to talk, you listen for more than 30 minutes +5
>
> You listen for more than 30 minutes without looking at the
> clock   +100
>
> She realizes this is because you've fallen asleep   -20

Couples, how do you rate on such a point system? Remember, wives, you can gain or lose points, also.

$Parting$ $Proverb$:

$Don't$ $murder$ $your$ $mate,$ $literally$ or $emotionally.$
$Rather,$ lay $down$ $your$ $life$ for $your$ $mate.$

NOTES

1 *Reclaiming Morality in America,* 1994.
2 Dr. Joe Harding, from a quote received through e-mail.

Reflecting on Lesson Six

1. Our ancestors believed that life is sacred. What does our society today appear to believe about life?

2. What did Jesus add to the commandment, "You shall not kill?" Why do murder and violence involve our heart?

3. How can our hatred destroy those about us?

4. What does criticism do to the spirit of its target person?

5. Explain why honesty and tenderness are keys to successful marriage.

6. What does neglect or indifference do to our family relations?

7. Why does Paul say that withholding sex from our mate is a violation of God's will for marriage?

8. How can failing to share in family responsibilities eventually erode your marriage?

9. Explain the damage that a habitual workaholic brings to marriage and family.

Consider this:

There is a common attitude among non-Christians in our society that men are inherently designed to have multiple sexual partners and that to expect marital fidelity is unrealistic and unfair. Do you buy this? Is monogamy-for-life possible? Some who espouse this promiscuous view insist that they don't know any husbands who have been 100% faithful and do not believe there are any or that they are extremely rare. What has been your experience? If you have never been personally affected by unfaithfulness, can you imagine what some of the destructive effects of such infidelity might be? If you have been affected, list some of the effects you have seen firsthand.

7

DO NOT FALL INTO AN AFFAIR

In this lesson:
- ▶ The twin ills of adultery and divorce
- ▶ God's covenant of marriage
- ▶ Reaping what you sow

God's Word:

You shall not commit adultery.

—Exodus 20:13

*But I tell you that anyone who looks at a woman lustfully
has already committed adultery with her in his heart.*

—Matthew 5:28

Today many married couples appear to have three licenses — one to marry, one to have an affair, and one to divorce at will. "After all," they say, "this man or woman I married turned out to be defective. I want a new model." So they shop around, their marriage vows meaningless.

The whole notion of marital fidelity "until death do us part" seems hopelessly Victorian in our age of individualism and self-realization. The principle of divine authority over our lives, including God's authority over our marriage, is out of place in the thinking of modern society.

> Today many married couples appear to have three licenses.

We consider ourselves a liberated age. Liberated from what? From the rules of our Creator, who knows far better than we will ever know what is best for our society, our family, and us. We fail to recognize that He has a prior claim on our lives. As Scripture says, "It is he who made us, and we are his . . ." (Ps. 100:3).

DIVORCE, TODAY'S CRIME AGAINST FAMILYHOOD

The result? One in two more recent marriages ends in divorce, according to figures released by such organizations as the Barna Group, the American Family Council, and Focus on the Family. Divorce brings with it broken homes, ruptured families, single-family dwellings, and children marked for life by the trauma of their parents' divorce.

I have watched a number of couples — even some of my own family — divorcing. Many of these divorcees are basically unhappy. The divorced woman, especially a mother, generally appears to suffer financial distress. Their children, who vow that they would never divorce as their parents have done, tend to replicate the same disastrous pattern.

SOME REASONS FOR DIVORCE

Divorce may occur for a variety of reasons. One major reason is economic — deep disagreement over family finances or the lack thereof. In some cases the marriage is shattered by an addicted spender or gambler. Divorce may occur because of different opinions over child-rearing. It may occur over sexual disharmony, infidelity, unrealistic work schedules, or being married to one's profession or pastime. It may be caused by abuse, drinking, drug addiction, contrary religious views, temperament differences, complaining, nagging, or widely differing social and cultural views.

A cartoon said, "Men are from Earth and women are from Earth. Live with it." However, it does appear that men and women are different in makeup and approach to life, and always will be. There are differences in physical, mental, and emotional makeup between the sexes. If we fail to recognize these factors that make us different from our mate, we may either attempt to force him or her to change or give up and head to a divorce attorney.

> The rather permanent "cure" of divorce may be no real cure at all.

Whatever the causes, the rather permanent "cure" of divorce may be no real cure at all. For the wife and mother, it may bring even more economic hardship, loneliness, the task of bringing up children alone, vulnerability, and other difficulties.

WHAT THE WORD SAYS ABOUT THIS

The Word of God is clear on the matters of adultery and divorce. Let us look first at adultery. God soundly condemns sexual infidelity.

For instance, "Marriage should be honored by all, and the marriage bed kept pure, for God will judge the adulterer and all the sexually immoral" (Heb. 13:4; see also Lev. 20:10; 1 Cor. 6:9; 1 Tim. 1:10).

Is there anything about these passages that we cannot understand? They are clear, are they not? Then why do we both commit adultery and condone it? Because we are easily tempted, because we rationalize our behavior, because we feel we got a bum deal in our marriage, because we are surrounded by sexual stimulation, and because we have unrealistic notions about love and sex.

Why such divine prohibition against a little sexual "adventure"? Not to thwart us, but to help guarantee a permanent marital union. The home is intended to be a bastion of security for both mates and for their offspring. The home is the bedrock of society. If that rock is shattered, Heaven help our society! Margie and I visited the Acropolis in Athens, Greece, before our Aegean cruise. The Parthenon and other structures atop it were built on a great rock mass. Had the Parthenon not been used as a munitions storage place and as target practice for cannon, it might still be nearly intact 2,500 years later.

> Marriage today often looks like the Parthenon in ruins.

Likewise, had it not been for infidelity and easily-obtained divorce, the home, created by God in the very beginning, might still be firmly grounded.

But, no, marriage today is on a fissured base of cultural expediency and it, too, often looks like the Parthenon — in ruins. We can only imagine the Parthenon's original beauty, just as we can only imagine the perfection of the marital union as God intended it. Yes, some couples reach fifty, sixty, seventy, or more years of faithfulness to their marital vows, but this may become a rarity when the present older generation is gone.

EASY GAME, BUT WITH DISASTROUS CONSEQUENCES

Adultery is an easy game to play but is something like Russian roulette. It can have dire consequences. In the workplace men are surrounded by beautiful, intelligent female colleagues, many of whom may be looking for a man and are not above enticing even married ones. Women, too, are in close contact with handsome, successful men and may easily succumb to an affair. Researchers report that office colleagues are often the most likely to be caught up in an affair.

> Adultery seldom goes undetected.

Adultery, however, seldom goes undetected. Sooner or later the betrayed spouse will find out, and it is a rare mate who is willing to forgive the adulterer and trust him or her again. One betrayed husband took his fallen wife back but constantly threw in her face, "Was he better in bed than I? Was he?" Adultery is a violation of everything marriage stands for in God's sight and in our society.

MARRIAGE STILL A COVENANT, NOT A CONTRACT

Marriage, I repeat, is a covenant, not a contract. Hear what our Lord says about this matter of covenant marriage:

[Wisdom] will save you also from the adulteress, from the wayward wife with her seductive words, who has left the partner of her youth and ignored the covenant she made before God (Prov. 2:16-17).

You flood the Lord's altar with tears. You weep and wail because he no longer pays attention to your offerings . . . You ask, 'Why?' It is because the Lord is acting as the witness between you and the wife of your youth, because you have broken faith with her, though she is your partner, the wife of your marriage covenant (Mal. 2:13-14).

The marriage covenant is entered into in partnership with God. He has always denounced covenant breakers because they undermine the foundation of our entire relationship with Him, as well as with each other.

> The marriage covenant is entered into in partnership with God, who has always denounced covenant breakers.

ADULTERY DESTROYS RELATIONSHIPS

Adultery does destroy relationships and none more than with the betrayed mate. The sacredness of marriage is smudged — dragged through the mud of an affair. This kind of emotional mess is nearly impossible to clean up. As in the case of Edgar Allen Poe's *The Telltale Heart*, our misdeed catches up with us.

There may be many causes for adultery besides lust of the moment. One is lack of sexual satisfaction in the marriage bed and loss of romance in the marriage. Compared to an indifferent and perhaps unkempt wife, career women may look very attractive and even sexy. The husband who is an avid sports fan, a couch potato, a poor provider, a verbal and/or physical abuser, or an addict may be setting up his mate for an affair with someone who is attentive to her. Two appropriate sayings come to mind. One is from the "ancient" Fred Allen radio show. Digby O'Dell, the friendly undertaker, often said, "The grass is always greener on the other fellow." Of course, this doesn't have to be true because there is another proverb, "If you keep your own pasture green for your stallion, he is not likely to seek greener pastures."

ADULTERY'S HARVEST

Adultery is a hell in itself. If unrepentant, those who succumb to it will be condemned to eternal Hell. Adultery violates all that is sacred, undermines our society and wreaks all kinds of damage to the hearts of others.

Not only that, an adulterous liaison is seldom permanent. Even if it brings about divorce and remarriage to the new partner, the entire social and spiritual base for this union is flawed. Our Lord clearly states that the new marriage is adulterous (Matt. 19:9).

> An adulterous liaison is seldom permanent.

Look very carefully, then, before you leap into an affair. There is a deep abyss of shattered lives and heartaches down there. It isn't worth the cost by any standard! It is smart, very smart, to avoid temptation by being extremely careful in your association with those of the opposite sex.

Parting Proverb:
Don't ever pick forbidden fruit. It will sour in your stomach.

Reflecting on Lesson Seven

1. What are the three licenses we looked at in this lesson? What is the basic error in the second and third licenses?

2. Why do you think long-term marital fidelity is out of place in our modern society? How does a lack of divine authority play a part in this situation?

3. Is divorce a crime against familyhood? How does it impact the couple and their children? What is the financial impact it carries with it in most cases?

4. What are some of the reasons given today for divorce? Is there any truth to the idea that men and women are basically different physically, mentally, emotionally, and even spiritually?

5. What does God's Word tell us about adultery? And about divorce?

6. Explain the difference between the concept of marriage as a contract and that of marriage as a covenant relationship.

7. Who is the senior partner in all covenant marriages? What is the spiritual consequence of breaking covenant with one's spouse?

8. How does the social crime of adultery catch up with us?

9. What are some causes of adultery? How can we guard against it?

Consider this:

One of the early lessons most parents teach has to do with property rights. We are not to take what belongs to someone else. If a playmate is playing with a toy, we mustn't walk up and take it away. Yet learning not to steal is a lifelong battle. We "borrow" a pen from the office intending to bring it back, but somehow it never gets from our pocket or purse back into our desk. In the same way, we are often guilty of stealing little things from our spouse. We don't think of it as stealing, but it is. Marriage mates should be equal partners in money, in sexual attention, in dignity, and in other areas. Consider ways we can steal from our partners and ask yourself if you are guilty. Then read lesson eight.

8

DON'T STEAL FROM YOUR MATE

In this lesson:

▶ Things we owe to our spouses and should not steal from them

God's Word:
You shall not steal.
—Exodus 20:15

He who has been stealing must steal no more . . . .
—Ephesians 4:28

"I, a thief? Not on your life! I have never stolen anything . . . except perhaps for some little trinket here or there, or a bit from Uncle Sam on my tax return."

This is probably a confession we could all make. I remember several petty thefts in my own life. I was working as a college student in the stockroom of a large department store. Bulk candy was kept in a topless cage. Well, I soon learned that the guys swiped candy from it by hoisting someone down headfirst into the cage, to scoop up a fistful of candy. Since I was the lightest in weight, guess who became the cat's paw? Right. One other time I found a necktie on the floor at the store and took it. I'm not proud of that little pilfery.

A movie years back was entitled *Never Steal Anything Small*. The story dealt with the audacious idea of stealing — not the contents of a bank, but the entire bank building by jacking it up and rolling it away. You and I would never be that daring. Yet, as suggested above, we steal in small ways, such as taking home company items from our office.

STEALING FROM OUR MATE?

Whether we realize it or not, we may also steal from our mate. How so? By robbing him or her of dignity, a good name, a fair share of the family's goods, proper dress, care, faith, protection, or even your due as a bed partner. Let us take a closer look at each of these points.

> A mate's self image can be whittled away until it no longer even exists.

Dignity

A mate's self image can be whittled away until it no longer even exists. A certain man belittled his gentle wife, who quietly took his abuse. She internalized it, but it didn't go away. It surfaced in frequent migraine headaches and other health problems.

No unresolved tension in a marriage lies forever dormant. Sooner or later it comes back to life with a vengeance. Constant criticism of our mate, in public or in private, does not correct the real or perceived defect; it just makes the matter worse. The Word tells us men, "Husbands . . . be considerate as you live with your wives, and treat them with respect as the weaker partner . . ." (1 Pet. 3:7).

What has ever happened to husbandly chivalry? I must confess that I have something of the "big chief" in me. Habitually I walk ahead of Margie on the way to a store or the car. Bad scene. There is probably no wild bear to combat on the trail ahead. We seldom see men any more pulling out a chair for their wife or female companion, opening a door for her, assisting her up and down stairs, and in other ways treating her gently.

Dignity is the name of the game — dignity in how we treat our mate in all circumstances. Harshness, cruelty, profanity, crudeness, thoughtlessness, and general ineptness have no place in marriage.

Our Mate's Share of the Family's Goods

Prenuptial contracts have little or no place in sound Christian marriages. "What's mine is yours, and I will share it if I can" should be the standard for all marriage partners. The husband who begrudgingly hands his wife an allowance is not fit to be married to her. On the other hand, a wife who goes through money as if it were

> Prenuptial contracts have little or no place in sound Christian marriages.

water is not worthy of her husband. And when the day of our death arrives, our surviving mate should receive at least the bulk of the family estate, all things being equal.

Proper Dress and Care

Men, your wives need to look well groomed out in public. Even in private, there is little excuse for her to spend her days resembling Eliza Doolittle before her transformation in *My Fair Lady*. And you wives should expect your husbands to be clean and reasonably well groomed in public, to say nothing of his life at home. I personally regret that our casual generation has lowered clothing standards so much in public. Dressing up for a play, concert, musical, wedding, funeral, public worship, dinner out, or other special occasions makes them more memorable and in good taste. We had a family rule when our children were still at home: "No shirt, no dinner." And as we presented ourselves before God in worship, we expected a degree of good taste in dress from our family. We had a struggle in Brazil over dress. The rage during our 18 years there was T-shirts with a message, generally in English, on the front. Some Brazilian teenagers showed up for worship in shirts that had an immoral message on them. Since it was in English they didn't really understand the hidden or not-so-hidden meaning. Our grooming does say much about us. Our clothing doesn't have to be expensive, but should be clean and appropriate for the occasion.

Caring for your spouse includes not only grooming, but seeing to hair care, toiletries, and other personal items. We need to pamper our mate in every way possible. This will pay rich dividends in our marital relationship.

Faith

It is best for the couple to be of the same faith and active in it. If you and your mate are united in the same faith, and I pray you are, then you should practice your faith together. Although no spouse can worship, pray, or engage in Christian activity in place of the other, yet we should reinforce each other's religious participation in every possible way.

Now if the marriage is divided religiously, it has its own set of problems. We have all seen "church widows" bringing the children alone to class and worship.

> We should reinforce each other's religious participation in every possible way.

Norman Rockwell illustrated this in his own insightful way with a *Post* cover showing Mom and the kids marching out well-dressed to services and glaring at Dad, who sits sloppily dressed in pajamas reading the paper and sipping his coffee.

If this is your state, you still owe your church-going mate every consideration in his or her faith. If both of you are active, but in different churches, this can become complicated, tending to polarize the children into one or the other parent's "camp." It requires much patience and understanding to deal with such a situation. If one or both are ardent in their own faith, they will attempt to convert the other, which may succeed in some cases, but in other cases creates even more tension.

Protection

We owe our spouses, and especially our wives, protection from danger, undue fears, and stresses. Margie has always said, "You can criticize me if you want, but you'd better not attack my family." She means it. I have seen her seriously defend her family.

The husband has a special obligation to protect his wife and family, even if it means taking a bullet to protect them. "Women and children first" should be every husband and father's credo in moments of real or perceived danger. And that doesn't mean pushing them into harm's way.

Sexual Consideration

Paul tells us that we owe our mate his or her due sexually:

> The husband should fulfill his marital duty to his wife, and likewise the wife to her husband. The wife's body does not belong to her alone but also to her husband. In the same way, the husband's body does not belong to him alone but also to his wife (1 Cor. 7:3-4).

Yes, it works both ways. Traditionally, husbands have expected sex on demand. Wives have the same right. However, neither one has the right to marital rape. The man owes his wife personal hygiene, tenderness in their sexual relationship, and a loving, caring way of behaving every day. She, in turn, owes him cleanliness, a good appearance, tenderness, and acceptance. She has every right to initiate sex, and how this will turn her man on!

> The right to sexual attention works both ways.

Parting Proverb:
Steal nothing from your mate. Rather, give everything in your power.
This will greatly enrich your marriage.

Reflecting on Lesson Eight

1. Suggest some ways in which we may steal from our company, school, or society in general.

2. Is it possible to steal from our own mate and family?

3. How do we sometimes go about stealing away the dignity of our mate?

4. How do some mates steal the other's share of the family's resources?

5. Do we owe our spouse decent dress and physical appearance? Should we maintain certain standards for our dress and that of our family in public?

6. How do some mates steal the faith of their marriage partner? How can they undermine the faith and religious practice of their family? Who should be the spiritual leader of the family?

7. Do we owe our mate and family a sense of protection and security? On whom does this primarily fall?

8. How do we sometimes steal sexual consideration from our mate? Is the body of the husband or wife his or her own property or does each belong to the other? What does Paul say about sex and sexual abstinence in a marriage?

9. Why is it important to give everything in our power to our mate and family?

Consider this:

The next lesson tackles the tricky issue of lying. Do you excuse lying on the basis of "tact" or consider that some lies are worse than others? When you told a "little white lie" out of "kindness," were you ever found out? What was the result? How do you maintain honesty in a marriage without brutality? Are there other forms of dishonesty in a marriage relationship besides outright lying? Be honest with yourself about your degree of honesty.

9

DON'T LIE TO OR ABOUT YOUR MATE

In this lesson:
- ▶ Little white lies?
- ▶ Misrepresenting each other
- ▶ Other forms of deception

God's Word:

You shall not give false testimony against your neighbor.

—Exodus 20:16

Do not lie to each other, since you have taken off your old self with its practices and have put on the new self . . . .

—Colossians 3:9-10

We tend to catalog lies according to their seriousness or type. "A little white lie" we consider appropriate in certain situations. For instance (and watch for this one), we respond to our spouse's question about her appearance, "No, you look great!" The truth may be that we have misgivings about her selection of wardrobe, jewelry, makeup, or hairstyle. How can we answer truthfully without hurting her feelings? This may take many years of trial and error to work out. Great tact is called for in attempting to be truthful without being blunt or heartless with the truth.

> Great tact is called for in attempting to be truthful without being blunt or heartless with the truth.

We may also be tempted to lie (a white lie, of course) about how we spent some time or money. If it is money spent for a surprise gift for her, it can be pretty tricky to get around the matter without stretching the truth. If it is something we spent on ourselves without advising our mate, it can be much more serious.

Or, there may be other failings we want to cover up, interfering with honesty and openness between spouses. I have learned over the years to just tell Margie, for instance, "Sorry, I forgot to call in that prescription."

"How could you when you wrote a note to remind yourself to do it?"

"I don't know. I just forgot!"

In earlier years I would have raised a small barrage of excuses about why I didn't do it. Now, no matter how much my forgetfulness may irritate her, I try to tell her the truth without a smokescreen to hide my failing. After all, I have a right to be forgetful; I'm a senior citizen. They say the second thing that goes is memory. I forget what the first thing is.

DECEPTION IS A SLIPPERY SLOPE

Another point about honesty: Its opposite, deception, is a slippery slope. I have never been good at it. Any time I have ever tried to deceive or even manipulate, it has always backfired. Deception can be a subtle thing, often attempted by just withholding some of the truth or allowing others to jump to a wrong or distorted conclusion.

Honesty is by far the best policy. It doesn't require all the "infallible" memory and trickiness that lying and deceiving do. Once we have embarked on a path of deception, especially to our spouse, there is no graceful way to get off of it. One lie may call for more to cover up the first one. When we are caught in a deceiving mode, others lose confidence in our integrity.

LYING ABOUT OUR MATES

We can lie to our mate and family. We can also lie about them. This untruthful tack may be in the form of exaggeration, boastfulness, criticism, shifting the truth just slightly, or just plain fibbing.

How many husbands have told some inviting beauty that their wives just don't understand them? They may paint a false or partially false picture of their mate in order to elicit sympathy. Or they may exaggerate the qualities of their

> We can not only lie *to* our mate and family but lie *about* them.

mate, in order to impress others. Both of these ways of behaving are forms of deception, aimed generally to manipulate those about us.

Bearing false witness comes out very clearly in marital problems, separation, and divorce. Margie and I have counseled various couples facing such a situation. The stories we have heard from "her" are a gulf apart from those we have heard from "him." Like the blind Hindustanis examining an elephant from their own perspective and coming to far different conclusions about the nature of the animal, so mates at odds with each other have stories they may truly believe, but their reality may not be all that real. When they are made to sit down and face each other honestly, both are usually found, like the blind Hindustanis, to be partially right and partially wrong. It is dangerous to hear and accept only one side of the story without giving equal attention to the other side.

> It is dangerous to hear and accept only one side of the story.

If all couples realized that they look at their mates through tinted glasses for better or for worse, this might help them reconcile their view of each other.

BAGGAGE BROUGHT TO MARRIAGE

Each mate brings to marriage his or her own worldview — a long-developed, but not articulated, set of assumptions, values, and allegiances. One great hurdle to cross in the marriage relationship is to understand these foundational views of the spouse without trying to force a change in the other. When we understand what assumptions about life our mate has, what values are built on these assumptions, and what loyalties these values trigger, we can be much more patient in living with that person. After all, we bring our own particular assumptions, values, and allegiances into marriage, and ours may not make that much sense to our spouse.

It is a serious mistake to determine, but not reveal, that once married, we will reform our new bride or groom. A recent commercial shows a young fiancée looking at her man's living quarters. She admires him and them outwardly, but has a vision of changing everything, right

> Having a hidden agenda of wanting to change the mate is a form of deception.

down to the books he reads, the TV shows he watches, the decor of the apartment, his dog, his car, and, although unstated, him as well.

This kind of hidden agenda is a form of deception. We marry for better or for worse, and sometimes, it is much worse than we imagined. Prince Charming may really turn out to be Pete the Pig.

DECEIVING OUR MATES

Deceiving our mates — we can do it in a thousand ways. Some women have been known to fake a loving attitude and even sexual satisfaction, when they really feel little or nothing. It might be better in the long haul to be kindly open about the matter. There may be a solution once the problem is known.

Deceiving our mates — we men are masters at hiding a feeling of sexual inadequacy or some other physical problem. We may have to be nagged into a medical checkup. After all, we're macho men. To us, it's a sign of weakness to admit we have a problem.

Lying to or about our marriage partner is a foundation of sand on which to build our marriage. Let us make sure that our speech is open and lovingly honest in all circumstances.

Parting Proverb:

If we are prone to lying or deception, what we really need is a spiritual heart transplant, for out of the heart comes such behavior.

Reflecting on Lesson Nine

1. Lying has become epidemic in our country. Why do you suppose this is?

2. Does the Bible differentiate between "white lies" and "black lies" or any shade in between? Why, then, have we categorized them according to our evaluation?

3. Can lying be more than just a wrong statement? Explain how it may include withholding all the truth, manipulating the facts, distorting the information, or allowing others to jump to a wrong conclusion.

4. How is deception related to lying? Give an example.

5. We can lie to our mate and family. Explain how we can also lie about our mate and family.

6. We used the expression "worldview" in the lesson. Of what is it composed at its heart? How can differing worldviews create problems in marriage?

7. List some baggage that we may bring into our marriage without even realizing it.

8. Why is it so dangerous to carry into a marriage a hidden agenda of determination to reshape our mate?

9. How does deceiving our mate endanger the very foundations of our marriage? Why did we suggest that lying to or deceiving our spouse is a foundation of sand?

Consider this:

Your neighbor has just bought a new car. It is beautiful. You look at your ten-year-old, scarred-up clunker and ask yourself, "Why can't I get a new car, too?" Well, why can't you? You can't steal your neighbor's car. If you go out and buy a new car, you may be stealing from your spouse or from your future or from your children's future. Yet if you dwell on your envy, the temptation to do something about it may become overpowering. Before looking at lesson ten, ask yourself, "How do I deal with lust?" If you don't have an answer, perhaps you need to take time to develop one before you find yourself in a position where lust has taken control of your mind and overpowered you.

10

DON'T BE GUILTY OF LUSTING

In this lesson:

▶ The sexual climate of our society
▶ Unrealistic expectations
▶ Where lust leads

God's Word:

You shall not covet your neighbor's wife . . ..

—Exodus 20:17

Put to death, therefore, whatever belongs to your earthly nature: sexual immorality, impurity, lust, evil desires and greed, which is idolatry.

—Colossians 3:5

So much in our society seems to point, sooner or later, to sex. Sexual innuendoes and explicit sex fill the screen. Sex is used to sell everything, even cars and tires.

Margie and I recently returned from a 50th-anniversary cruise to the Aegean, thanks to our family and a host of friends. In looking at art and sculpture from ancient Greece the thought struck home strongly that the Grecian culture was obsessed with and worshiped the human body, just as our culture today. Yet neither their idolatry nor their explicit sexual graphics saved them. Everything in their ancient history, from gods to girls to gardens, is a heap of ruins.

WHERE OUR SEX-CRAZED SOCIETY IS HEADED

Is this where our sex-crazed society is headed? Will they wonder about our civilization when they dig it up one day? Will Golden Arches be displayed in some future museum as some sexual or cultic icon of the 20th century? Will our pornographic

> Will Golden Arches be in some future museum as a sexual or cultic icon of the 20th century?

material be unearthed some distant day and be pondered? During our cruise we saw explicitly pornographic pictures and culture, in ruins but still graphic. Is this really what we want for our culture?

OUR PURSUIT OF THE ALMIGHTY DOLLAR

Will our temples devoted to sex, power, and the almighty dollar be pieced back together some day? In the movie, *Planet of the Apes*, the clincher came at the end of this futuristic space story. The solitary, upraised arm of the Statue of Liberty reached out of the sand along the sea — a relic of a destroyed civilization.

Pornography, even child porn, is big business, and even when it is not totally pornographic, suggestive sex reigns on the media. Sitcoms, talk shows, and the late-night specials appear to be built around sexual topics.

All of this assault on our sexual appetites only makes them worse. We see handsome men and gorgeous women on TV and in films mating outside the sanctity of marriage or portrayed in adulterous relationships, even when the story line does not need such gratuitous behavior.

What does this do to our psyches? We become drugged with sex, absorbing more and more of it as it becomes more and more perverse. This says nothing about the coarse language in the media. A friend commented to me recently about an otherwise very good film, "There was some profane language in it, but

> That we no longer blush may be a sad commentary on the extent to which we have become desensitized.

we no longer blush at such expressions." This may be a sad commentary on the extent to which we have become desensitized.

PREOCCUPATION WITH SEX

What does all of this tell us?

It causes us to be preoccupied with sex and coarseness. We expect and demand it. Our bedroom sex life perhaps has never been as frequent as opinion polls and books indicate, so this makes us vaguely dissatisfied. Frequency is not nearly as important as quality. Because we are so sex-oriented, we may expect perfect performance from our mate. This is altogether unrealistic. Babies, tiredness, distractions, and our own lack of kindness and consideration all enter into the sex chemistry. Such things as lack of privacy may dampen our performance, especially that of the wife. Illness, health problems in general, and aging may drastically interfere with sexual fulfillment.

So we see titillating sex all about us and compare our own sex life with it. Often, I fear, the comparison leaves our mate appearing to be a sexual underachiever. We see that along with our spouse growing older and more wrinkled, he or she has also experienced a diminishing sex drive. While this is all natural with aging, our youth-oriented society will not tolerate it. Perhaps it is time to trade that old "model" in for a newer one. . . .

A POOR MARRIAGE HAND

We begin to feel that fate has dealt us a poor marriage hand. This makes us vulnerable. So along comes a comely neighbor's wife, a friend, a colleague at the office, or even a relative. Since we feel cheated, we long for an exciting new adventure. If we really want it, sooner or later it comes along. We begin to lust after that "chick" or "stud," and the first thing we know, we have "fallen" into an extramarital affair. An affair is so easy to fall into, but extremely difficult to correct and make amends, hopefully to restore our marriage. All too often this is an impossible task. Our mate feels that once we have cheated, we can never again be trusted.

So it's goodbye marriage and, probably before long, goodbye fling also. Or perhaps we fall into the trap of serial marriage — one mate after another as we search for that "perfect one."

Jesus tells us that not only is adultery wrong, what precedes it is wrong. If we even look at that man or woman lustfully, we have already committed adultery in our hearts (Matt. 5:27-28). The thought comes before the deed. Reason, which should rule our mind, is knocked out of the driver's seat by emotion.

FALLING INTO SEXUAL TRAPS

Let's say, however, that we have never seriously entertained having an affair. We can still fall into one without realizing what is happening until it is too late. We work and travel day after day with that person who appears to be much more interesting than our own partner. We eat out together while on business. We tempt fate and fate wins. How could it have happened? How, indeed!

Our lusting may never take the form of an affair. We may substitute the fantasy of pornography or sexual daydreaming. Pornography, so easily available, may easily become addictive. The more of it we absorb, the more we want.

> Our lusting may never take the form of an outward physical affair.

In my limited exposure to it — and who can miss it when traveling in countries where extremely explicit sexual scenes are for sale at any magazine stand — pornography paints an unreal and perverted view of sex. By comparison our own sex life may seem dull.

In addition, pornography degrades both the females and the males portrayed. They are made out to be play toys instead of real people. Pornography can ruin marriages and even lives. Appearing to be an "innocent" pleasure, it is a consuming fire of desire.

CAREFUL ABOUT LUST

The Lord tells us not to even look lustfully at someone other than our spouse. Even more, we are not to covet anything belonging to others — not their mates, homes, cars, SUVs, boats, wardrobe, electronic gadgets, pro- fession, position, popular- ity, athletic prowess, or anything else about them.

> We are not to covet anyone's mates, possessions, position, popularity, or anything else.

A tough assignment this is in our highly competitive, sexually driven, and materially oriented society. So be it. The Lord still knows what is best for us and what is worst. Let us take His orders seriously.

Parting Proverb:
Don't pant after another pair of pants, male or female.

Reflecting on Lesson Ten

1. Would you agree or disagree that our culture today is sex-oriented? If so, why? If not, why?

2. Can we become drugged with sex until it becomes not only a passion, but also an addiction? How does our constant absorption with sex deaden our consciences?

3. When we see exciting sexual figures and situations all about us, especial- ly in the movies and on TV, what can this do to our marriage?

4. What can lead us to feel that we have been given a poor marriage hand?

5. If we attempt to make up for feeling cheated in our marital relations by turning to pornography or an adventure with someone else, what can this do to us, to our mate, and to our marriage?

6. Is it possible to ever truly make amends for an affair? Can we ever be trusted again by our spouse?

7. What are some sexual traps into which we can fall? How can we guard against them?

8. Surely we all understand how lusting after another person is sinful. What do you think about lusting after things, profession, position, popularity, athletic ability, or other things you do not have?

9. Why should we take the Lord seriously about His instructions on sexual adventures, fornication, adultery, and lusting in general?

Consider this:

These ten commandments are the basics for a solid foundation in marriage, but just as God gave Moses many, many other laws which demonstrated how the first ten commandments could be worked out in day-to-day living, so are there other rules to consider in our day-to-day relationship with our spouse. Skim the headings in lesson eleven and think about how they apply to your marriage before reading the lesson.

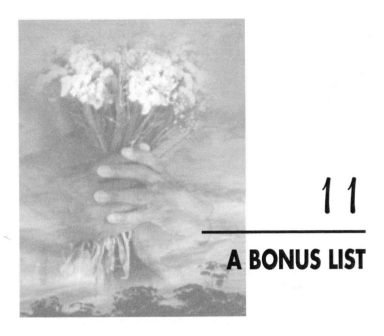

11

A BONUS LIST

In this lesson:

▶ More principles of fairness, communication, perspective, humor, and sharing

Following are two bonus lists of "commandments." These can be used as eleventh and twelfth lessons for a thirteen-week course or just as enrichment suggestions for helping you grow a better marriage. Some of these cover points not covered in the ten preceding "commandments."

Writer Sue Ellin Browder lists several rules for a happy marriage.[1] We will adapt them to our Christian theme in this book.

DO NOT OPT OUT OF SOLVING MARITAL PROBLEMS BY "FIGHTING FAIRLY."

Fighting fairly means listening carefully to the other person, paraphrasing what was said, and then presenting your own case. There is one serious problem with this, Browder says: It seldom works. Psychologist John Gottman notes that "for 80 percent of couples, active listening is too hard." Fighting "fairly" does not guarantee a happy marriage. Loving well may be a far better aid to marriage — not just sexual love, although that is important. God's Word says that a truly loving marriage is based on *agape* love and not just on *eros* love, from which we get the word erotic. *Agape* love is that level which seeks the good of the other with no thought of self or of love in return.

> Fighting "fairly" does not guarantee a happy marriage.

DO NOT ASSUME THAT SILENCE MEANS EITHER AGREEMENT OR EXCLUSION.

During more than 50 years of mostly very successful marriage, my reaction to points of conflict between Margie and me has been to retreat into a shell of silence because I hate confrontation. I still do, but I am slowly becoming better able to handle the "hot buttons" in our marriage. "When you marry, you automatically inherit a set of unresolvable relationship problems," Dr. Gottman says. "If you married someone else, you'd have a different set."

Of course, we should live at peace with each other, but if we try to solve every difficulty, we may end up spending our time picking at these rather than building on our strengths. Margie and I will never agree on some subjects, but we now realize we don't have to. Dis-

> Disagreement, even silence, doesn't necessarily mean rejection.

agreement, even silence, doesn't necessarily mean rejection.

LOVE YOUR DIFFERENCES.

As we have noted already, men and women are different in many respects. As the French say, "Vive la différence!" For this reason couples bring into their marriage different inborn temperaments, personalities, and life experience. They are different in worldview. That is, they have different basic assumptions, values, and loyalties. The very characteristics that attracted us in the first place to our mates should be celebrated, rather than criticized.

DON'T SWEAT THE SMALL STUFF.

We seem to somehow survive major traumas. Dealing with little annoyances may be like the little foxes of Scripture that spoil the vines (Song of Solomon 2:15). How to discipline the kids, how to share housework, what and how much TV to watch, how to spend money, how to handle the in-laws, and how much emotion to show outwardly — friction over these things is what often rubs marriage the wrong way.

LAUGH.

If both husband and wife can laugh at their own and mutual foibles, they are on their way to building a strong marriage. If they can face their differences with humor, says Browder, they can relax and enjoy life together. The long view of life together with a chuckle or two along the way can put many a difference in perspective. If they can look at their differences objectively, there may be some real humor in them.

PUT YOUR HEADS TOGETHER . . .

and you may come out ahead. When couples work together to solve difficulties or to plan their life together, they may find solutions that neither one would have thought of alone. Not only this, each one may complement the other. I'm a dreamer, a risk taker, not always very practical and somewhat impulsive. Margie is more pragmatic than I. She thinks things through more carefully and holds me in check. In turn, I hopefully encourage her to have a greater vision.

STAY CONNECTED.

Couples must take time to be alone together. We attempt to keep Friday nights just for the two of us. We can't always do this, but most Fridays we do. We also plan two or three days alone on our anniversary. This doesn't guarantee that we have solved all of our communication problems, but it helps. We don't converse as much as we should on a daily basis, but we are working on it. Well, right now

> Couples must take time to be alone together.

I'm typing this book instead of talking to her. I have a way to go yet. Do you?

TAKE A LEAP OF FAITH . . .

and believe everything will turn out for the best. Dr. Steven J. Wolin, co-author of *The Resilient Self*, says, "It requires a leap of faith to believe this in our age of divorce, but it's crucial for turning hardship to strength."[2] Believing things will work out for the best very often greases the wheels for a positive outcome. We took a long leap of faith when we decided, right after marriage, to take on an assignment in Dallas, another to

> Believing things will work out for the best very often greases the wheels for a positive outcome.

do mission work in Brazil, another when we accepted work in Abilene, Texas, and then when we accepted positions here in Oklahoma City. Right now we're taking a leap of faith in pledging to help construct a large new church facility. But leaping in faith is good spiritual exercise.

RELIVE BEAUTIFUL MOMENTS.

Margie and I have many such moments to recall and relish. We have been richly blessed, not necessarily in income, but in many other areas. Our lack is not in having memories. It is in our failure to take time to enjoy them together. All families need traditions, but they also need to appreciate and nourish their traditions. The Lord told Israel that its spiritual and national traditions were to be preserved and protected. We should do the same for positive family traditions.

Here they are then, ten (OK, nine) more "commandments" for couples. This isn't all, however. Turn to Lesson 12 for more.

Parting Proverb:
Get your exercise by serving your mate and family, and by building great family traditions.

NOTES

1 *Reader's Digest,* Nov. 1999: 100-104.
2. Dr. Steven J. Wolin, *The Resilient Self* (New York: Villard, 1993).

Reflecting on Lesson Eleven

1. What do you think about the practice of "fighting fairly" in a marriage?

2. Does silence mean agreement with our spouse's position? Are there any relationship problems or points of view that are truly unresolvable? Why or why not?

3. Why should we love the differences in temperament, worldview, and lifestyle between our mates and us?

4. How are little daily annoyances often more dangerous to marital relations than some major crisis?

5. Why is it important for a couple to laugh together and play together?

6. Why is it important to work together to solve difficulties and plan life as a couple?

7. What can couples do to stay connected to each other?

8. Why is it important to believe that things will work out for the best?

9. How can we improve our marriage by reliving beautiful moments in our marital and family history?

Consider this:

Does your mate go out of his or her way to look nice in public? Do you consider this a reflection on you? Does his or her good taste or poor grooming say that you have good or poor taste? When your spouse makes the effort to do nice things for you, do you let him or her know how much you appreciate it, or do you just accept it as your due? Do you take an interest in your mate's spiritual growth, or do you consider that between him/her and God? Pray about these attitudes before tackling lesson twelve.

12

YET ANOTHER LIST OF COMMANDMENTS

In this lesson:
> ▶ Separate rules for her, for him, and for the couple

During our years in Brazil we saw a great need for premarital counseling, so we took courses and did a lot of reading in order to respond to this need. Out of our attempts at counseling came a list of rules for women, one for men, and another for both.

FOR THE WOMAN OF THE HOUSE:

☞ Do not defile your body with excessive food, tobacco, or alcohol, that your days may be long in the house which your husband provides for you.

☞ Put your husband first before your mother, father, daughter, or son, for he is your lifelong companion.

☞ You shall not nag.

☞ You shall not undermine the self-respect of your husband in public or in private.

☞ Permit no one to tell you that you are having a hard time of it and should get out of your marriage. Neither your mother, sister, neighbor, colleague at work, nor friend at church shall be permitted to undermine your marital relationship.

☞ You shall not withhold affection from your husband, for every man loves to be loved, accepted, and respected.

☞ Do not forget the virtues of cleanliness and modest attire.

☞ Remember that the frank approval of your husband is worth more to you than the admiring glances of a hundred strangers.

> The frank approval of your husband is worth more to you than the admiring glances of a hundred strangers.

☞ Keep your home in good order, for out of it come the joys of your old age.

☞ Honor the Lord your God all the days of your life, and your children will rise up and call you blessed.

FOR THE MAN OF THE FAMILY

☞ Do not mess up your body and your life with tobacco, beer, drugs, junk foods, and lack of proper exercise.

☞ Make your wife the queen of your home, honoring her and defending her.

☞ Do not insult, yell at, or abuse your wife in any way.

☞ Do not let anyone else undermine your relationship with your wife or her good name, nor tell you that you have a hard time of it with your wife.

☞ Do not withhold affection from your wife, nor be overbearing with your manner. Be kind and gentle to her.

☞ Do not forget to take regular baths and keep yourself well groomed, even in a casual setting.

> Honor God all the days of your life. Your wife and children will rise up and honor you.

☞ Forgive your wife with grace, for who among us does not also need grace and forgiveness?

☞ Remember that the approval and even adulation of your wife is worth more than the approval of a hundred strangers.

☞ Keep your home in good repair and your yard in good order. They speak volumes about you. A place in good order brings contentment to your mate.

☞ Honor God all the days of your life. Your wife and children will rise up and honor you.

NOW FOR BOTH OF YOU:

☞ Do not attempt to escape your differences. Discuss them, if possible, but only in a calm, unhurried moment.

☞ Do not guard up in your heart all of the complaints you have against your spouse.

☞ Attack the problem, not your spouse.

☞ Deal with facts, not accusations. Do not throw at your mate all your "garbage" collected over the years.

☞ Offer possible solutions, not criticism.

☞ Keep a cool head, not an emotional one. Try not to dramatize, shout, or cry.

☞ Never exaggerate, such as "You always . . ." or "It's your problem." A cartoon I saw recently comes to mind. The husband sees his wife doing a slow burn and says, " I can't stand to see you so upset, Honey, so I'll be in the next room if you need me."

☞ Avoid comments about your mate's appearance, weight, clothing, or parents unless he or she requests input. Even then, walk and talk with great caution.

☞ Do not manipulate your mate by saying, "No, it was all my fault," or "If you give in to me this time, I'll do something good for you sometime. Or even, "If you will just do this for me . . ."

> Do not manipulate your mate.

☞ Be humble. You just might be in the wrong or at least partially in the wrong. Usually there are two sides to every marital conflict.

Don't stop here. There is still a wrap-up to come, so turn the page.

Parting Proverb:
Make your mate the king or queen of your home.
Treat him or her as royalty, not a serf.

Reflecting on Lesson Twelve

1. Why must wives put their husbands ahead of all others, except for the Lord?

2. What is the danger in allowing others to side with you in a marital difficulty?

3. What does every husband need from his wife apart from sexual pleasure?

4. Why should a wife expect her husband to care for his body, avoid any kind of addiction, and eat and exercise properly?

5. Why is it important for the husband to keep the home and yard in good condition?

6. Why should marriage partners respect the differences in temperament, background, and experience between them?

7. Why is it important to deal with facts in a marriage, rather than emotional responses and accusations?

8. Explain why it is important for mates to avoid negative comments about each other, or to avoid saying, "You always . . ." or "You never . . ."

9. Is it true that there are two sides to a marital difficulty? If so, why do we not listen carefully and prayerfully to our mate's side in the matter?

Consider this:

Did you take this class because it's what your Bible school class or small group was studying? Are you looking at these lessons because you wanted to improve your marriage? Why you took the class can make a difference in whether or not it helps your relationship with your spouse. For the last twelve weeks you have looked at various "rules" which, if applied to your marriage, should make it more solid. Have you applied any of them? Has your spouse? If you haven't up to now, are you ready to get serious and really look at your marriage honestly and make some changes? Is your spouse hoping you are? You can treat the wrap-up that follows as a thirteenth lesson or just make the pledge on your own, but it is for people who are really serious about making their marriages work

WRAP-UP AND A PLEDGE

What have we learned in these lessons? Let's think about it.

First and foremost, we live by law, whether we like it or not. There are laws that govern our lives as citizens and there are laws that govern our lives spiritually. There are rules for living a healthy life. There are also rules for successful marriage. Some of these we have considered in the "commandments" covered in this book. Those who live outside the law are anarchists. Marriage anarchists ignore the rules and end up both paying the price for their folly and exacting a high price from others.

WRAP-UP

Commandment 1

LOVE GOD ABOVE YOUR MATE — AND YOUR MATE AS YOURSELF

In Commandment 1 we discussed loving God above your mate and your mate as yourself. Only with a sound set of priorities, with God first, Christ second, our mate third, and ourselves fourth, can we hope to succeed in any aspect of life (1 Cor. 11:3). How do we go about keeping the Lord on the throne of our hearts and at the head of our table? Ponder this carefully and answer in the space provided.

_____

_____

_____

How can we place our mate — husband or wife — ahead of us in preference and esteem?

_____

_____

_____

Commandment 2

SMASH THOSE IDOLS!

In Commandment 2 we discussed the need for destroying the idols in our marriage. Idols are anything that we place above God or in competition with Him. What idols have you battled in your life?

_____

Describe how they have distracted you from your devotion to God and the spiritual quality of your marriage.

_____

_____

Discuss ways in which you can smash the idols in your life and marriage.

_____

_____

Commandment 3
DON'T BADMOUTH YOUR MATE

Badmouthing others, and especially our mate, is a recipe for disaster. What effect does continual criticism have on its target?

_____

_____

How can you go about bathing your marriage in the oil of love and consideration, rather than harshness?

_____

_____

_____

Commandment 4
HONOR YOUR MATE'S SPECIAL DAYS

Christians have various advantages over non-Christians. What are some of these?

_____

_____

Why do Christians normally rally to specific crises and needs?

_____

Why should we be very alert to the needs and crises of our mates, to say nothing of his or her special days?

_____

_____

Commandment 5
HONOR YOUR PARENTS AND EACH OTHER

In today's casual society respect for others, especially older people, has largely faded away. Yet, God still requires us to honor our parents and our mates.

How can you go about creating a climate of respect for authority, for the elderly, and for your mate?

_____

_____

Commandment 6
DON'T EVEN THINK ABOUT MURDERING YOUR MATE

There are many ways by which to murder others. We can murder their reputation, criticize them, judge them, and condemn them.

Where does Jesus say murder begins? _____

Rather than murdering your mate emotionally, how should you be treating him or her?

_____

_____

_____

Commandment 7
DO NOT FALL INTO AN AFFAIR

Affairs are easy to fall into but disastrous in their results. Deep hurts, scandal, and divorce are some of the more obvious consequences. Others may be severe financial stress and children damaged, perhaps permanently.

How is divorce today's crime against familyhood? _____

_____

How do you plan to "affair-proof" your marriage? _____

_____

_____

What can you do to greatly reduce the chances of divorce in your own marriage?

_____

_____

Commandment 8
DON'T STEAL FROM YOUR MATE

As in the case of murder, so it is with stealing. We may never literally steal an object belonging to our mate, yet may be guilty of thievery — dignity, rightful possessions, proper dress and care, faith, protection, and sexual consideration.

Have you been guilty of belittling your mate or cheating him or her out of due care and consideration? _____ If so, how can you proceed to undo such theft?

_____

On the contrary, what do you owe your mate?_____

_____

_____

Commandment 9
DON'T LIE TO OR ABOUT YOUR MATE

Lying involves more than just telling an outright untruth. It involves evading the truth, manipulating the truth, deceiving, and permitting others to come to a wrong conclusion from what we said or withheld.

How can you improve the quality, accuracy, and truthfulness of what you say to your mate?

_____

_____

How can you accomplish this and at the same time use tact and diplomacy in what you say?

_____

_____

Commandment 10
DON'T BE GUILTY OF LUSTING

Lasting marriage cannot be built on a foundation of sex or lust alone, for sexual drive will diminish and lust is a transitory emotion. True love is the only foundation on which to build a lasting marital relationship.

How can you avoid falling into sexual traps at your work, social engagements, or even church activities?

_____

_____

How can you develop in your own life and marriage *agape* love?

_____

_____

A PLEDGE

Read and prayerfully consider this marital pledge. If you accept it into your marriage, please sign the pledge below. If not, will you write one that you and your spouse can accept and follow?

We, _____ and _____ _____ ,
pledge to God and to each other that:

1. We will place the Lord on the throne of our lives and our home.

2. We will rid ourselves of all idols that we have placed above God, on a par with Him, or in competition to Him.

3. We will take great care never to badmouth each other, especially in public.

4. We will meticulously strive to honor each other in every possible way, especially in the realm of birthdays, anniversaries, and other special occasions.

5. We will honor in every possible way our mutual parents as well as each other.

6. We will treat each other at all times with care and kindness.

7. We will scrupulously guard against any possibility of an affair.

8. We will never knowingly steal each other's good name, reputation, share of family possessions, or right to our attention, sexual and otherwise.

9. We will not knowingly lie to or about each other, nor will we deceive each other or withhold necessary truth from each other.

10. We will avoid, at all costs, lusting after some other person or some object not our own.

Signed on this _____ day of

_____, 20_____

_____   _____

       husband   wife

ABOUT THE AUTHOR

Glover Shipp is a professional journalist, writer, and artist, as well as a teacher and church elder. He has served, taught, and lectured in 45 countries. For 18 years he was a codirector of publications for the Escola da Biblia and Editôra Vida Cristã in Brazil. He also engaged in general mission work, editing a regular evangelistic magazine and writing a number of books and courses in Portuguese and Spanish.

Among his books is the previous College Press publication, *Marriage Is a Covenant, Not a Contract*. He has taken courses in pastoral counseling and family relations, and has counseled couples before and after marriage. He is also licensed to administer and evaluate temperament analysis tests.

Dr. Shipp brings to his writings experience in a number of fields besides family and marriage counseling. He has graduate degrees in communication, missiology, theology, and urban anthropology, and has taught courses in World Religions, Comparative Doctrines, Islam, African Roots of Spiritism, and Urban Anthropology & Evangelism, as well as a number of other ethnic and language courses. He is also a published poet and hymnwriter.

He has been married for 54 years this September (2002) to the former Margie Smith, who is recently retired from Oklahoma Christian University. He is the father of six children and grandfather of 13. He is the son of a preacher and the grandson and great-grandson of elders.